Derby
TROLLEYBUSES

Colin Barker
Series editor Robert J Harley

MP Middleton Press

Cover picture: Sunbeam 239, bound for Osmaston Park Road, takes a left turn at the junction of St Thomas Road and Walbrook Road before tackling the steep climb of the former to reach the Barracks and then onwards to the Mitre. (C.J.Barker)

Published November 2001

ISBN 1 901706 72 9

© Middleton Press, 2001

Design David Pede

Published by
        Middleton Press
        Easebourne Lane
        Midhurst, West Sussex
        GU29 9AZ
Tel: 01730 813169
Fax: 01730 812601

Printed & bound by Biddles Ltd,
        Guildford and Kings Lynn

CONTENTS

INTRODUCTION AND ACKNOWLEDGEMENTS

I was born in Derby and lived in the area until 1991, spending my childhood years in the Normanton district during the 1940s. My mother and I frequently used the trolleybuses to the town centre from St Thomas Road and the Cavendish and hence developed a lifelong interest in the rest of the Derby system and trolleybuses in particular. Three childhood events sparked this interest.

The first was following a wartime visit to my grandmother's in Hastings where the single deck trolleybuses of Hastings Tramways caught my attention. Imagine my surprise when returning to Derby and leaving the Midland Station at being confronted by an identical vehicle. It was of course one of the six purchased secondhand by Derby from the Hastings Tramways Company.

The second was as a result of another wartime visit, but this time to Nottingham. Having previously seen that city's green and cream trolleybuses, I was completely taken aback by the sight of a blue and cream trolleybus just around the corner from Old Market Square. Who did it belong to and where was it going? I subsequently found the answers to be Notts and Derby Traction and Ripley.

Finally, imagine my childhood excitement when having discovered one could identify the make of chassis by the tax disc, I was able to establish the regular dinner time workman specials to the Cavendish were a Karrier, a Sunbeam, a Ransomes Sims and Jeffries and a Brush-Thornycroft.

This photographic journey takes the reader along the roads of this railway city, which was served by trolleybuses for over 35 years. It does not profess to be a detailed history, as this has been adequately covered in other publications. Whilst the contents will be of interest to those who study public transport, I hope it will bring back nostalgic memories to a wider audience who travelled on the system on a regular basis.

A few words of explanation are required on the arrangement of the photographic sequence. I have worked outwards along each main route from the two central termini, namely the Market Place and Victoria Street, and have endeavoured to minimise views seen in other publications.

Whilst route numbers were allocated and used fairly diligently prior to the commencement of the abandonment programme, once this process began there was a marked deterioration. As routes were closed, renumbered and those remaining combined to give optimum scheduling, the disciplines on route numbers and destinations became lax. Therefore on many later views the destination/route number does not appear to relate to the location; I have not endeavoured to comment on this in the text.

The photographs chosen originate from a wide variety of sources with many taken by individual enthusiasts. Where the photographer or organisation is known, due credit has been given. Inevitably some views give no indication as to their originators, but I hope they will accept that their work has been chosen with good intent in order to enhance this publication for a wider audience.

Thanks go to Philip Thomas and John Simpson for use of views from their comprehensive photographic collections. Also to Philip Thomas and to Barry Edwards for their helpful suggestions having read through the draft text. I would also like to thank Robert Harley for his guiding hand on this, my first venture into publication and my wife, Maureen, for her support and word processing skills.

Finally, as a 60th birthday surprise, I was able to drive preserved Sunbeam 172 around the Sandtoft Museum circuits; it only seems like yesterday when as a child I travelled on newly delivered 172 with a strong smell of varnish eminating from the wooden slatted seats.

GEOGRAPHICAL SETTING

Derby sits at the very beginning of the Pennine range with the flat Trent Valley to the south and east and the beautiful Peak District to the north and west. The steepest gradients for trolleybuses were St Thomas Road, Browning Street and Sinfin Lane on the southern routes plus sections of Burton Road. The River Derwent runs through the centre of the city before joining the River Trent at Shardlow to the southeast.

Derby was granted County Borough status in 1888 and city status in 1977. It is an important railway city where routes from the Northeast to the Southwest/South Wales meet the St Pancras line from London.

It is also an important industrial city that includes Rolls Royce and Adtranz the train builder (to be purchased by Bombardier) whose heritage goes back to the time when Derby was the headquarters of the Midland Railway.

HISTORICAL BACKGROUND

The first horse-drawn bus service in Derby commenced around 1840 from the newly opened railway station to a number of hotels in the town. In 1877 other operators introduced a modest network of services mainly feeding the railway station. The Derby Tramways Company, formed to operate horse trams in the Borough, bought out private operators in 1880. The first horse tram route was opened in March 1880 and ran from the Market Place to Midland Station via London Road. The system rapidly expanded with an eventual fleet of 20 horse trams and a route mileage of 4.7 miles (7.56km). A number of horse buses continued on less patronised routes.

Derby Corporation exercised its powers to purchase the private company in 1899, taking over on 1st November. The Corporation obtained an Act of Parliament in 1901 to electrify the system and introduce new/extended routes. The first electric tram ran on 27th July 1904 and the last horse tram finished on Ashbourne Road on 1st June 1907. At its peak the system had almost 14 route miles (22.53km) with only 3.25 miles (5.23km) single track. The last of the 78 tramcars purchased was delivered in 1927, but a need for heavy capital expenditure on the system plus the growth of new housing beyond the tram routes, led the Tramway Committee to consider trolleybuses.

The Derby Corporation Act of 1930 allowed for the introduction of trolleybuses and the full Council's confirmation of the Tramway

Committees recommendation allowed the conversion to proceed.

The first route was Nottingham Road where a combination of equipment deterioration, a new river bridge, depot access and a need to extend beyond the tramway terminus gave it high priority. Whilst conversion took place, motorbuses ran the route for 14 months, but trolleybuses took over on 9th January 1932. Conversions and extensions of routes then took place rapidly with Market Place-Alvaston (Wyndham Street) on 24th July 1932, Market Place-Osmaston Road (Allenton) on 13th November 1932, Uttoxeter and Burton Roads on 13th August 1933, Ashbourne Road on 31st December 1933 and the Normaton/Pear Tree routes on 18th March 1934.

An extension was built from Normanton (Cavendish) to serve Old Normanton and a new council housing estate around Browning Street. This replaced regular short workings to the Cavendish and was opened on 30th January 1935.

In 1935 the Corporation wanted to extend the Kedleston Road motorbus route to the end of Allestree Lane, which was on the western fringes of the village of the same name. The Traffic Commissioner refused this extension so the Corporation exercised their trolleybus running powers with start up on 28th April 1935.

A major extension took place on 29th November 1936 when the St Thomas Road and Osmaston Park Road motorbus mileage was converted to trolleybus with short workings available at the Barracks and Victory Road. On the same date a branch off the Nottingham Road route was introduced along Chaddesden Park Road into the rapidly developing housing in this area.

Two more extensions took place before the outbreak of war, these being along Duffield Road to the entrance to Darley Park on 11th July 1937 and the Osmaston Road extension from Allenton to Shelton Lock on 6th November 1938.

Trolleybuses served Derby well during the war years aided by some secondhand vehicles from Hastings and utility vehicles delivered towards the end of hostilities. Derby suffered only minor bomb damage, bearing in mind the importance of Rolls Royce in the town, unlike other Midland towns such as Coventry. A number of factories were located in Sinfin Lane and on 30th August 1943 this route was opened for trolleybus operation.

On 14th September 1947 the Duffield Road route was extended to the eastern side of Allestree village at Kingscroft. Post-war housing development gathered pace with Chaddesden expanding rapidly plus a large new estate off Ashbourne Road at Mackworth. Additional motorbus routes served Chaddesden, which led to the withdrawal of the Chaddesden Park Road route from 11th November 1950, although wiring was left for special journeys. The Mackworth Estate was however served by trolleybuses and the Ashbourne Road route was extended in two stages from Kingsway to the junction of Ashbourne Road and Prince Charles Avenue (8th June 1952) and along Prince Charles Avenue to Morden Green (26th July 1953). With the wiring along Ascot Drive for depot access this was the last route extension giving a maximum mileage of just under 28 miles (45.05km).

In March 1952 it was found that a culvert under the north side of Victoria Street was in danger of collapse. The Normanton group of routes were moved to the Market Place and the eastbound overhead slewed to the centre of the road for through routes from Uttoxeter Road and Ashbourne Road. This arrangement remained until November 1957.

On 31st January 1960 the Browning Street route was extended and converted to motorbus and the overhead from the Cavendish removed.

The next abandonment was the original Nottingham Road route, which ceased on 10th November 1962, although trolleybuses then took over majority control of the Sinfin Lane route having previously been a mixed trolley/motorbus operation. Exceptions were during Victoria Street culvert repairs (motorbus) and the 1956 Suez crises (trolleybus).

In July 1963 the decision was announced to abandon trolleybuses altogether, although six new vehicles were delivered in 1960. Burton Road and Duffield Road routes last ran on 3rd October 1964 and Sinfin Lane on 1st January 1966, although occasional journeys continued on the latter until wiring was removed. Uttoxeter Road, Cavendish to Midland Station finished on 26th November 1966 and Kedleston Road on 11th February 1967 with the remaining routes succumbing at the final closure of the system on 9th September 1967. So ended over 35 years of trolleybus operation.

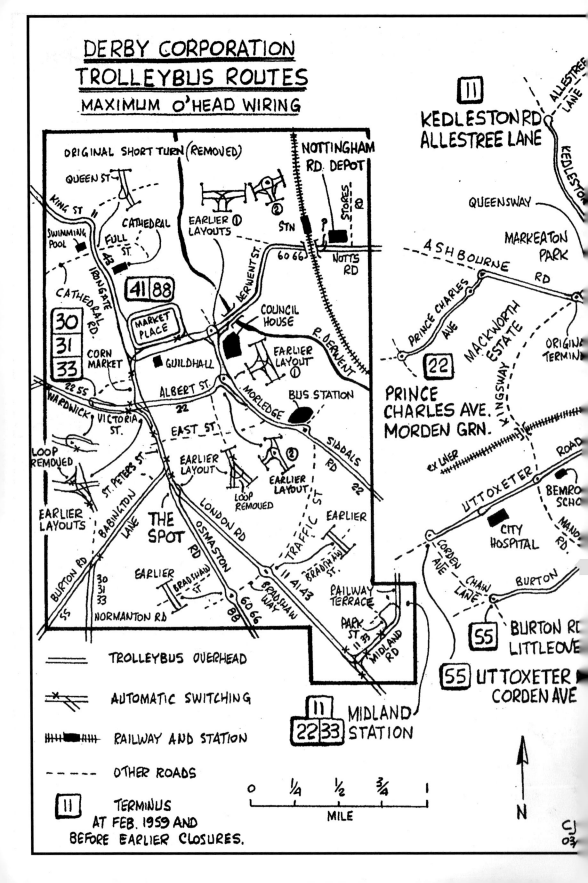

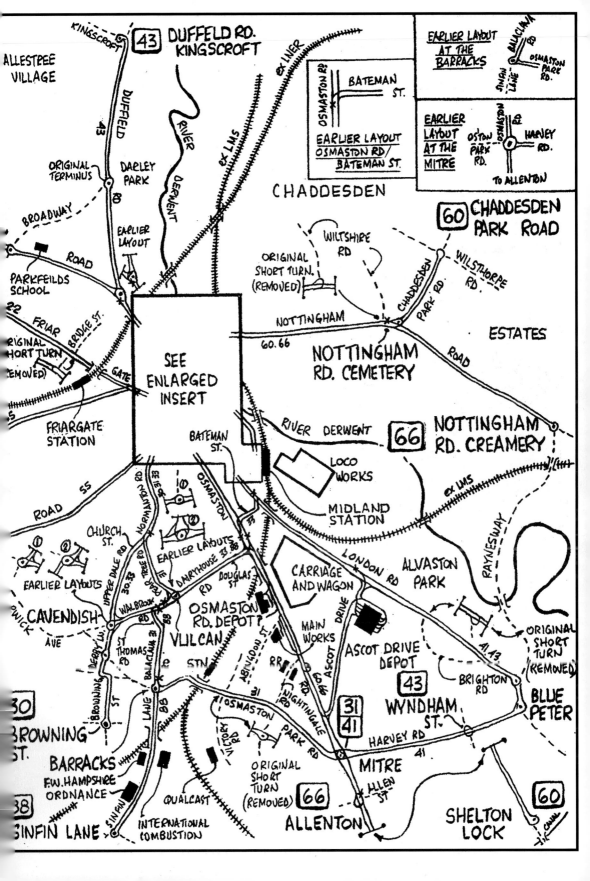

EXTRACTS FROM AN ARTICLE BY THE
GENERAL MANAGER, P W BANCROFT, PUBLISHED IN 1933

On March 31 1933, the first complete year's running of the new vehicle was completed and the results so far justified the decision made. With receipts at 17d per mile and working expenses at 11.5d there is a balance sufficient to pay not only the capital charges on the system but also the loss on the tramcars; also the capital charges included a full year's repayment of capital on vehicles which have been in service in some cases as little as four months.

The type of vehicle adopted was a 56 seater double decker on a six-wheeled chassis, and measuring 27ft 6in overall. A 75 hp motor has been employed to give rapid acceleration and Westinghouse air brakes on four wheels in the earlier models and on six wheels in the later models, give ample braking. As the vehicles run outside the borough on unlighted or partially lighted roads an auxiliary electrical system is included, with a dynamo run direct on the front end of the main motor.

It is difficult to judge the effects of conversion on receipts, as in no case has a tramway been replaced by a trolley bus service over exactly the same length of route and the same service, but the following figures for the Alvaston Route, with for 16 weeks was fairly comparable with the corresponding period of the previous year, show an increase in takings of 19 per cent.

Experience has shown the necessity for a first-class overhead line, and we have never made the mistake of attempting to use a tramway line with minor modifications and the addition of a negative wire. The work, carried out partly by contract and partly by the Department's own staff, has been carefully planned throughout, turning circles, curves and junctions laid carefully to drawing, and even curves of large radius on open roads have been studied from the point of view of the normal position of the vehicle, and all new wire and fittings have been used throughout. The result has been that, even through the initial stages with inexperienced drivers - and all our drivers have been trained from tramcar drivers - trolley booms have never caused any serious trouble.

The overall schedule speed, which with tramcars was approximately 7 mph, has been raised by trolley buses to 9.4 mph, which is higher than that obtained by the motor buses on the town services.

The trolley bus has gained the goodwill of the public and has recovered the traffic which the tramway had lost, and the Corporation is sufficiently satisfied with the results to accelerate the conversion and has decided to complete the replacement of the tramway services during the financial year.

TROLLEYBUS PREVENTATIVE MAINTENANCE
MAINTENANCE CHECK LIST
c1937

GROUP A
Examine brushes and commutators on Traction and Westinghouse motors. Renew brushes where necessary. Clean brush holders. Examine Westinghouse switch, governor, leads, etc. Check all lights and switches at full voltage. Check action of air bells from all pushes. Grease Westinghouse motor bearings at three-monthly intervals.

GROUP B
Top up all batteries, clean terminals and tops. Examine low tension wiring for insulation. Check all low tension circuits for working wiper, horn, buzzer, emergency lights, direction indicator and ammeter. Check dynamo for charge as bus moves out. Grease traction motors and oil Flettner ventilators at three-monthly periods.

GROUP C
Clean, grease and check all trolley bases. Examine trolley leads, radio coils and terminals. Make good all damaged tapes. Check tensions. If these are less than 33lb or more than 37lb notify the fitter accordingly.

GROUP D
Examine all contactors and main controllers. Clean and grease contacts, lubricate spindles slightly ahd check pig tails. Look out for wear on controller spindles. Check correct sequence of fingers making contact with shunt barrels. Verify all power terminals for tightness. Examine trunks in driver's cab for defective insulation.

GROUP E
Examine all brake linings for wear. Check action of hand brake. Examine Westinghouse brake for build-up, noise, application and release. Examine brake pedal and spring. Clean, oil and examine leaves of front springs. Clean steering mechanism, grease and check all parts for tightness.

GROUP F
Lubricate rear bogie, cardan-shaft, universal joints and Westinghouse compressor. Clean and oil rear springs. Examine brake drums for oil. Examine differentials for leakage. Generally examine chassis and grease all brake pivot points.

TRAMS TO TROLLEYBUSES

1. Guy 84 from the original delivery turns the southwest corner of the Market Place whilst on test. In addition to running on trade plates 120 CH there is a large "On Test" notice in the rear nearside window. The tram driver looks on, perhaps wondering when his training will start on the new type of vehicle. (Derby Museums)

2. The official end to the tramway system was the 2nd July 1934, although the last services had finished on the 30th June. The last delivered tramcar 78 poses in Victoria Street with Guy trolleybus 127 in the background. (Courtesy of Derby Evening Telegraph)

3. The tramway style livery can be clearly seen in this early view of one of the original Brush bodied Guys parked on the west side of the Market Place on what was to become the Alvaston stand. The buildings to the rear were demolished to make way for the new Assembly Rooms. (W.J.Haynes)

4. Dodson bodied Guy 94 is parked on the south side of the Market Place in the immediate post war period. The Guildhall is immediately behind and the Weights & Measures Office was once the Police Station before the erection of new buildings in Full Street. (R.Marshall)

5. Guy 103 with Weymann bodywork turns into the Market Place to reach the Shelton Lock stand. 103 was withdrawn in 1949; this photograph was therefore taken in the period after the war. Modern modular overhead crossovers and junctions have replaced original wooden insulators. Wartime blackout markings are evident on the standards and the Council House is in the background. (R.Marshall)

6. An incident in winter snow - Guy 147 is depicted opposite the Nottingham Road stand between the Market Place and Corporation Street. The scene is immediately after the war as evidenced by 147 and the Sunbeam utility to the rear left still being fitted with trolley wheels as opposed to carbon skates. (C.J.Barker collection)

7. Daimler 162 in lined out livery unloads before turning into the Market Place. In the background is the Council House, which was started in 1938 but not completed until 1948 because of the war. The area behind 162 has been made into a public open space after lying derelict for many years. (R.Marshall)

→

8. Sunbeam W 181 stands on the north side awaiting departure to Sinfin Lane. Daimler 162 is on the Allenton/Shelton Lock stand to the rear. Front fleet numbers were moved to the drivers cab door on subsequent repaints. The old Assembly Room façade on the left is now at Crich Tramway Museum (recently rebranded Crich Tramway Village). (A.B.Cross)

→

9. The driver of Sunbeam 200 has misjudged his driving line in trying to gain the Kedleston Road stand on the western side of the Market Place. This overhead was only used for special journeys other than in the early years of the system. The driver of 208 returns to his cab after helping out. (J.G.Simpson)

10. Roe bodied Sunbeam 242 leans over whilst turning round the east side of the Market Place on the Sinfin Lane service and with the Christmas tree on display. The Guildhall, rebuilt after a fire that occurred in 1841, is on the left; all this is now a traffic free pedestrianised area. Austin products abound on the car park. (C.J.Barker collection)

(top right)

11. The Kedleston Road/Duffield Road routes headed north from the Market Place and shared wiring to the Five Lamps junction, which Sunbeam 198 is approaching. The view looks back along Duffield Road towards King Street with the Cathedral Tower in the background. (J.G.Simpson)

(lower right)

12. After a dewirement, or having taken the wrong overhead line at the Five Lamps, Sunbeam 215 manoeuvres under battery power to gain the correct line for Duffield Road on the right. In the centre background is Kedleston Road. The conductress stands with bamboo retrieval pole to the ready. (R.Cox)

13. Sunbeam 218 turns out of Kedleston Road and around the Five Lamps island on its way to the Market Place and onwards to the Midland Station. The place name originates from when there was an elaborate Victorian structure, which carried five gas lamps. Although they have long since gone, everyone still refers to this area as the Five Lamps. Duffield Road continues to the rear of 218. (J.G.Simpson)

14. The conductor releases the handpull for the junction at the Broadway/Kingsway island on Kedleston Road, whilst Sunbeam 237 completes its turnback for the town centre. It will probably travel a short distance before parking to await the pupils from Parkfield Cedars Girls School. This junction is now covered by a bridge over a dual carriageway. (J.G.Simpson)

15. Utility Sunbeam W 179 has left the Allestree Lane terminus of the Kedleston Road route abou half a mile (0.80km) away and makes its way towards the Broadway/Kingsway island. This rout was originally intended to be operated by motorbuses, but the Traffic Commissioner refuse permission. Trolleybus powers were therefore exercised to gain access to this lucrative suburba area. (R.G.H.Simpson)

16.   Willowbrook bodied Sunbeam 230, resplendent in its original livery with cream rear roof, is pictured at the Allestree Lane terminus. Vehicles turned at the junction of Kedleston Road/Allestree Lane; the latter is in the left background and leads into Allestree village. (C.J.Barker collection)

17.   Sunbeam W 180 turns at the Duffield Road/ Broadway island, which was the original terminus of the Duffield Road route prior to the extension to Kingscroft in 1947. Broadway, on the right, was the northern end of the incomplete ring road, and the entrance to one of Derby's parks is along Darley Park Road on the left. (P.J.Thomas)

18.   On the opposite eastern side of Allestree village was the terminus of the Duffield Road route at Kingscroft. 219 is seen at this picturesque turning circle, which was the location of many post war official photographs. The site is now occupied by private housing. (R.F.Mack)

NOTTINGHAM ROAD/CHADDESDEN PARK ROAD

19. Sunbeam 237 negotiates one of the two bridges on the Derby system, which carries the railway line north to Sheffield and Leeds over Nottingham Road. The station of the same name was to the right of the bridge with the entrance on the opposite side from this view. The original road level can be seen on the right, being lowered part width on the left when the bridge was built. This section was lowered twice for trams and full width for trolleybuses with the resulting dip filling with water whenever there was heavy rain. A few yards further on was the entrance to Nottingham Road Depot that closed in 1949. (P.J.Thomas)

20. Both routes shared overhead to Cemetery junction and here Sunbeam W 173 turns out of Chaddesden Park Road into Nottingham Road on its return to the depot, having worked out from Nightingale Road. Although regular scheduled services along Chaddesden Park Road ceased in 1950, workman specials continued until 1962. The Cemetery junction short working wiring can be seen coming in from the left. (P.J.Thomas)

21. Sunbeam 241 is seen at the turning circle on Chaddesden Park Road, which was at the Margreave Road/Wilsthorpe Road junction. Housing on the vast Chaddesden estates was private and council built both before and after the Second World War. However, this was very much motorbus territory and the route was the only incursion by trolleybuses. (A.D.Packer)

22. Roe bodied Sunbeam 238 stands at the Nottingham Road Creamery terminus prior to returning to Shelton Lock. The Derby ring road never fully circled the town and the island in the background was the eastern end of the incomplete circle. The then Trent/Barton territory of Spondon lies beyond the island. (Photobus)

(top right)
23. All routes going south from the Market Place travelled down the short length of the Cornmarket. A busy prewar scene is depicted with two of the Dodson bodied Guys making their way to St Peters Street. Moving into the Market Place is another trolleybus followed by a double decker motorbus and one of Derby's three trial diesel single deckers. (C.J.Barker collection)

(lower right)
24. This is a rare shot of the Brush-Thornycroft trial vehicle 114 in service and on its way to Allenton in the early years of operation. Route 65 was from the Market Place to Allenton as opposed to the through running route 66 from Nottingham Road Creamery to Allenton. This vehicle spent long periods out of service. (W.W.Winter)

25. Four vehicles, led by 211, ascend the Cornmarket before crossing over Victoria Street/Albert Street junction and then into St Peters Street. It is the end of the evening peak and the first and third vehicles are depot bound. All are Sunbeams and the bodybuilders represented in the first three are Brush, Willowbrook (based on Brush design) and Roe. (J.G.Simpson)

26. Sunbeam 240 has just crossed the Victoria Street/Albert Street junction to enter the Cornmarket from St Peters Street. The building to the right was originally the Royal Hotel; the rooms opposite with the circular windows, and those immediately below, were once an annexe to the hotel. (J.G.Simpson)

VICTORIA STREET

27. Brush bodied Guy 120 about to leave Victoria Street and turn right into St Peters Street and thence onward to Midland Station. This view was probably taken in the first half of 1934 with tram track and overhead still in place and the trolleybus overhead into Albert Street (to the right of the picture) not yet installed. The road to the right of the Royal Hotel is the Cornmarket. (W.W.Winter)

28. Guy 139 on the north side of Victoria Street in 1950 awaits departure to Osmaston Park Road, having turned round at the island to the rear of the tower wagon. The tower wagon is a Tilling Stevens B20; it had previously been a searchlight unit with the War Department and was purchased in 1948 and fitted with a tower ex Salford Corporation. (A.B.Cross)

29. Daimler 161 in wartime livery with white front stripe/mudguards and masked headlights is parked on the south side of Victoria Street outside the original Congregational Church. If the destination is correct, 161 will turn at the western end of the street to reach the Littleover stand on the north side. (W.J.Haynes)

30. Sunbeam 202 stands on the north side of Victoria Street. The passing loop of overhead allowed vehicles from the Wardwick to overtake those on the Normanton stands. These wires were slewed towards the centre of the road, and the Normanton stands were moved to the Market Place when strengthening of the underground culvert took place between 1952 and 1957. (J.G.Simpson)

31. Utility Sunbeam W 184 turns at the western end of Victoria Street. The parallel set of wiring allowed vehicles turning here to overtake those on stand for departures along the Wardwick. This arrangement was introduced when the north side of the street was reopened after strengthening of the underground culvert. Prior to this there was only a single set of overhead, which caused much de-poling. The modern Congregational Church is to the rear of 184. (A.D.Packer)

32. Confusing destinations on a hot day! 217 leaves Victoria Street to turn right into St Peters Street on route 33 to the Cavendish. The vehicle behind also shows route 33 and will carry straight on into Albert Street on its way to Midland Station. The original wiring had a branch from roughly above 217 into the Cornmarket to the right of the picture. This was removed by the end of the war. (J.G.Simpson)

33. The last three generations of Sunbeam trolleybuses are on view at the Victoria Street/St Peters Street Junction. Roe bodied 236 leads the departure from Victoria Street followed by Brush bodied 204 and Willowbrook bodied 224 bringing up the rear. The original overhead junction from St Peters Street into the Cornmarket on the right was suspended from the bracket arm in the foreground before being moved further back to provide parallel running. (J.G.Simpson)

ASHBOURNE ROAD / UTTOXETER ROAD

34. The Ashbourne Road and Uttoxeter Road routes left the western end of Victoria Street and shared wiring along the short distance of the Wardwick, where they parted. The Ashbourne Road service continued along Friargate, whilst Uttoxeter Road trolleybuses turned left into Curzon Street. Here 231 enters Friargate with the Lord Nelson pub in the background together with wiring into Curzon Street which, by the time this view was taken in 1967, was only used for electrical supply purposes. (P.J.Thomas)

35. Sunbeam 229 emerges from under the second of the bridges that had to be negotiated on the Derby system. This graceful structure, produced by local iron founder Handyside, carried the Great Northern (later LNER) rail line over Friargate into the station of the same name on the left. Horse tramway stables were underneath the railway arches on the right with the entrance on the far side. (R.Cox)

36. Sunbeam W 177, new in May 1946, and built to relaxed utility standards poses at Kingsway/ Queensway island. This was the original Ashbourne Road terminus and wartime road markings to help with the blackout can be clearly seen. Trolley wheels were fitted when delivered but this was the first vehicle to be fitted with carbon insert skates and was used on the Uttoxeter Road/Burton Road route during the trial period. The area to the rear is currently the entrance to Markeaton Park, but when the photograph was taken it was an army camp. (D.C.O.D.)

37. Sunbeam 218 has just turned off Ashbourne Road into Prince Charles Avenue; this was the turning point for the first extension into the Mackworth estate in June 1952. The livery is as delivered with black lining out below the upper windows. The Willowbrook bodybuilder's transfer can be seen below the triangular Sunbeam badge. (J.Fozard)

38. A rather battered prewar Guy 148 is seen at the same location in its last year of operation. This vehicle was delivered in 1935 and was withdrawn after 17 years service. Looking at the unfinished traffic island and roadside, the view was taken not long after the opening of the access roads into the Mackworth estate. (W.J.Haynes)

39. Sunbeam 204 ascends Prince Charles Avenue to the turning circle at Morden Green. The curved roads of the post war estate were not ideal for overhead layout and it has been stated that this was the reason trolleybuses never progressed further. In the background can be seen a following vehicle at the junction with Ashbourne Road. (C.H.Fletcher)

Ashbourne Rd. & L.M.S. Station	22	Ashbourne Rd. & Victoria Street	23
Victoria Street & L.M.S. Station	21	Ashbourne Rd. & Osmaston Rd.	28

ORDINARY FARES.

Ashbourne Rd. & L.N.E.R. Station	1d.	Merchant St. & L.M.S. Stn. (or Midland Rd.)	1½d.
Merchant St. & Albert St.	1d.	Victoria St.& Victoria St.	1½d.
Victoria St.& L.M.S. Stn. or Midland Rd. (via Siddals Rd.)	one way 1d.	L.M.S. Stn. & Merchant St.	one way 1½d.
L.M.S. Station &Victoria St.	only 1d.	Victoria St. & Ashbourne Rd.	only 1½d.
Ashbourne Rd. & Albert St.	1½d.	Ashbourne Rd. & L.M.S. Stn. or Midland Rd.	2d.

WORKMEN'S FARES.

Ashbourne Rd. & L.M.S. Station	1d.	Ashbourne Rd. & Arboretum St. ... 1d
Ashbourne Road & Nightingale Rd.	1½d.	

WORKMEN'S RETURN FARES.

Ashbourne Rd, & L.M.S. Station 3d.

Fare table -
April to October 1935

40. Willowbrook bodied Sunbeam 219 turns at Morden Green whilst on a special working. Another vehicle can be seen at the layover point prior to returning down Prince Charles Avenue to join Ashbourne Road. Housing construction is in full swing around what was the last trolleybus route extension other than for depot access. (C.J.Barker collection)

→

41. 209 turns back to town at Uttoxeter Road/ Manor Road island. Although this wiring was usually used by Bemrose School specials, on this occasion 209 was running late and had been asked to turn back at the City Hospital half a mile (0.80km) further on. With an empty vehicle the driver decided to gain a few more minutes by turning here. This junction is now a major crossroad controlled by traffic lights. (G.Thomas)

→

42. Brush bodied Sunbeam 201 turns back to town outside the City Hospital; the normal route carried on for a further half a mile (0.80km) to Corden Avenue. Just beyond this point the overhead had to be realigned during the war to accommodate a roadblock. (J.G.Simpson)

43. Sunbeam 221 is about to enter the turning circle at the end of the Uttoxeter Road route. There were proposals to extend the overhead approximately 0.625 of a mile (1km) to Cavendish Way, which would have brought trolleybuses to the edge of Mickleover. Note the Guy lorry in the background. (C.W.Routh)

(top right)
44. 234 has just passed under an automatic switched junction and two crossovers to enter Albert Street from Victoria Street in the background. Some problems must have been experienced since the trolley booms appear to be down. The culverted Markeaton Brook runs under Victoria Street and continues under Albert Street and the River Gardens to flow into the River Derwent. A Co-op Morris Commercial van turns into the Cornmarket. (Vectis)

(lower right)
45. This single deck Guy 165 dating from 1928, and parked outside the offices of the Derby Evening Telegraph in Albert Street, was one of six purchased from Hastings Tramways in 1942. Painted in war time livery with white lifeguard, front mudguard edges, wheel hubs, rear stripe and the name Derby omitted to confuse any enemy invaders, only four of these vehicles entered service and 165 lasted until 1945.
(Courtesy of Derby Evening Telegraph)

46. Sunbeam W 179 uses the short length of overhead along Corporation Street between Derwent Street and the Morledge. Apart from the early years of operation this wiring was used for special journeys to Nottingham Road (overhead removed in this view) and Kedleston Road. The Council House is to the right and Magistrates Court/Police Station to the rear. (J.G.Simpson)

47. 199 has just left Albert Street to the left of the picture and is entering the Morledge on its way to Midland Station. Corporation Street is to the rear of the PMT bus inward bound from Hanley. (C.J.Barker collection)

48. A circa 1934/35 view in the opposite direction looking down the Morledge to Cockpit Hill has Dodson bodied Guy 88 about to pass under the junction for Albert Street on the vehicle's left. Although the Albert Street wiring is in place, 88 will continue forward into Corporation Street and thence into the Market Place before going north along Kedleston Road to Allestree Lane. Subsequently vehicles turned left into Albert Street and then onwards to Ashbourne Road having arrived from Allestree Lane via London Road, Midland Station and Siddals Road. (W.W.Winter)

Sunday timetable - October 1939 - April 1940

L.M.S. STATION, KEDLESTON ROAD & ALLESTREE LANE
Route No. 11.

SUNDAYS.

ALLESTREE LANE TO MARKET PLACE AND L.M.S. STATION.
10.2 a.m. and every 20 minutes until 1.42 p.m.
1.57 p.m. and every 10 minutes until 10.7 p.m.
10.17 p.m., 10.27 p.m., 10.37 p.m. to Market Place only.

KEDLESTON ROAD (BROADWAY) TO MARKET PLACE AND L.M.S. STATION AND 'BUS STATION.
10.5 a.m. and every 20 minutes until 1.45 p.m.
2.0 p.m. and every 10 minutes until 10.10 p.m.
10.20 p.m., 10.30 p.m., 10.40 p.m. to Market Place only.

MARKET PLACE TO L.M.S. STATION AND CENTRAL 'BUS STATION
10.13 a.m. and every 20 minutes until 1.53 p.m.
2.8 p.m. and every 10 minutes until 10.18 p.m.

L.M.S. STATION TO MARKET PLACE AND ALLESTREE LANE VIA CENTRAL 'BUS STATION.
10.0 a.m. and every 20 minutes until 1.40 p.m.
1.55 p.m. and every 10 minutes until 10.15 p.m.
10.25 p.m. to Market Place only.

CENTRAL 'BUS STATION TO MARKET PLACE AND ALLESTREE LANE
10.4 a.m. and every 20 minutes until 1.44 p.m.
1.59 p.m. and every 10 minutes until 10.19 p.m.
10.29 p.m. to Market Place only.

MARKET PLACE TO ALLESTREE LANE.
9.46 a.m. and every 20 minutes until 1.46 p.m.
1.51 p.m. and every 10 minutes until 10.21 p.m.

49. Guy 140 moves along the Morledge towards Cockpit Hill and Siddals Road in 1950. Note the advertisement for the Grand Theatre on the hoardings. A small fairground was once situated to the rear of the hoardings. (A.B.Cross)

50. Roe bodied 240 is observed at Cockpit Hill opposite the 1933 bus station. This site used to be the location for many market stalls of which the best known was "Mad Harrys". All was demolished to make way for the Eagle Centre. (C.J.Barker collection)

51. Willowbrook bodied 217 swings around the island at the end of the Morledge before entering Siddals Road on its way to Midland Station. Cockpit Hill is in the left background and the Upper Deck Café of the bus station to the right. (R.Marshall)

ST PETERS STREET/THE SPOT

52. Dodson bodied Guy 93 is at the bottom of St Peters Street and is about to cross Victoria Street/ Albert Street presumably on its way to Nottingham Road depot via the Market Place. Tram track and overhead are still in place and two early motorbuses help complete the scene. The Marks & Spencer building on the left dates from the early 1930s. (B.K.Edwards collection)

53. 218 leads 209 out of Victoria Street into the bottom of St Peters Street amongst cars that would have pride of place at any rally. The road markings to the left provide two lanes, whilst the overhead wiring is single line. In later years the Victoria Street/Cornmarket overhead junction was moved higher up St Peters Street to provide parallel running. (R.Cox)

54. Daimler CTM 4 demonstrator was on trial in Derby for over six weeks in 1937. This smart vehicle had a Willowbrook 56 seat body and is pictured halfway down St Peters Street with the Babington Lane junction in the background. An order for six similar vehicles followed although with Brush bodywork. The registration is incorrect and should read CWK 67; it was eventually purchased by South Shields (234) and after wartime bomb damage it was rebodied by Roe. (C.J.Barker collection)

55. Guy 84 at the top of St Peters Street is just about to pass under the overhead junction for Babington Lane on the left. The Brush bodied vehicle is on route 44, which turned at the Mitre Hotel having travelled along Harvey Road. This arrangement was prior to the erection of overhead along Osmaston Park Road and St Thomas Road. St Peters Street was the most intensively used stretch of overhead wiring, being covered by all routes other than Ashbourne Road for the majority of the system's life. (W.W.Winter)

56. The Spot at the top of St Peters Street is where the routes along Osmaston Road and London Road parted. Sunbeam 201 leaves The Spot and turns into Osmaston Road on a depot run with an additional person in with the driver. London Road is on the other side of Easterns Store. The Spot was originally a Y road junction, but in the postwar era the triangular section in the centre, which incorporated underground public toilets, was made into a traffic island. (W.J.Haynes)

(top right)

57. Both the Burton Road and the Normanton group of routes used the short climb up Babington Lane before going their separate ways. Sunbeam 198, in as delivered livery, climbs after leaving St Peters Street at the bottom of the hill. The building on the extreme left was the Joseph Wright School built in the early 1860s. (A.B.Cross)

(lower right)

58. We arrive at the junction of Normanton Road and Burton road with 207 about to descend Babington Lane. The Burton Road route on the right has been closed, but some overhead has been left in place for electrical supply purposes. Behind 207 is Unity Hall erected in 1908 as a meeting place and headquarters for local trade unions. (A.D. Packer)

──────────────►

60. 226 is depicted at Chain Lane turning circle. The traffic island was created towards the end of the system's life and BICC overhead line hangers used. This company provided a last "job lot" of fittings before ceasing to produce trolleybus overhead equipment. Representations by the Electric Traction Committee of the Municipal Passenger Transport Association (of which John Frith, Derby's Manager was a member) to delay the cessation of production were to no avail, although the company did propose a final consolidated order for the then remaining operators. (C.Carter)

59. 228 on learner duty turns at the little used short working on Burton Road. Warwick Avenue is on the left of the traffic island and Manor Road to the right. The regular route carried on a further mile (1.60km) to Chain Lane, which leads to Corden Avenue. The Burton Road and Uttoxeter Road termini were therefore only half a mile (0.80km) apart. There were proposals to join the two but these were opposed. (R.Cox)

──────────────►

61. Sunbeam W 184 has just left the junction for the Burton Road route at the top of Babington Lane and is proceeding along Normanton Road, passing the end of Sacheveral Street, to the Normanton Hotel and then onwards to the Vulcan. The towers in the left background are the erstwhile Derby College of Art, which subsequently became a Technical College and then part of Derby University. (G.Thomas)

62. Willowbrook bodied 224 has operated the overhead automatic switch and is about to turn into Pear Tree Road at the Normanton Hotel. The wiring to the left leads to Lower Dale Road, Church Street and Upper Dale Road and onwards to the Cavendish. Slightly to the rear of 224 was the storage yard for Offilers Brewery; also in the background are the towers of the Methodist and Congregational Churches. (P.J.Thomas)

(top right)

63. Sunbeam 243 is at the Cavendish island on the last day of operation after having arrived from Midland Station via Walbrook Road. The destination Cavendish relates to a public house, which was originally a hotel. The Fine Fare supermarket site was once a cinema carrying the Cavendish name and the abandoned Browning Street route ran up Derby Lane to the left of the building. (R.F.Mack)

(lower right)

64. Two utility Sunbeams, 171 and 172, are parked just around the corner from the Cavendish Hotel in Walbrook Road. In the late 1940s this is where the "odd men out" - 99, 100, 101 and 114 - could be seen periodically on lunchtime workman's specials. (T.W.W.Knowles)

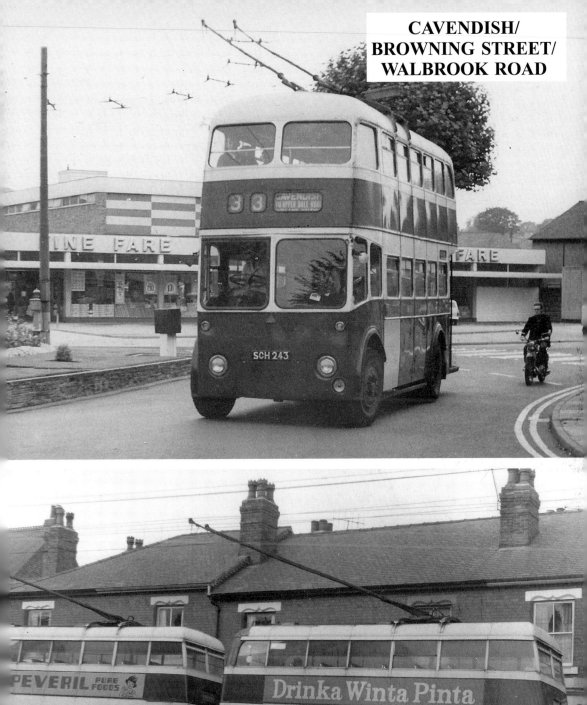

65. Browning Circle was the terminus of the Browning Street route. Brush bodied 214 is on service whilst Willowbrook bodied 234 to the rear is on an enthusiasts' tour of the system. The influence of the Brush style on the Willowbrook design can be clearly seen. (A.D.Packer)

(top right)

66. The Vulcan was where the wiring from Pear Tree Road joined those from Dairyhouse Road in the background. 175 takes the tight turn around the traffic island from Pear Tree Road and enters St Thomas Road. It is on service with a learner driver - standard practice in Derby. The wiring leading to the left immediately in front of 175 was hardly ever used other than for football specials in the late 1940s and early 1950s. Behind 175 once stood the Normanton Cinema, a regular haunt in the author's childhood days. (P.J.Thomas)

(lower right)

67. Having climbed Douglas Street from Osmaston Road, 212 is about to descend Dairyhouse Road to join St Thomas Road at the Vulcan. St James's Church School is on the right. (C.W.Routh)

PEAR TREE ROAD / ST THOMAS ROAD/DAIRYHOUSE ROAD/BALACLAVA ROAD

68. 220 has just passed under the overhead junction for Walbrook Road and is about to ascend the steeply inclined section of St Thomas Road. The Walbrook Road wiring to the Cavendish continues to the left. (P.J.Thomas)

69. 201 turns out of Balaclava Road (a continuation of St Thomas Road) into Osmaston Park Road on its way to the Mitre, where it will become route 41 and continue via Harvey Road/London Road to the town centre. Note the street furniture; the island has disappeared and this is now a major crossroad controlled by traffic lights. (J.G.Simpson)

70. The Barracks, home to the Sherwood Foresters Regiment, and where the two routes part company. 189 has just left Osmaston Park Road and is about to enter Balaclava Road before dropping down St Thomas Road. The Sinfin Lane route drops sharply by the side of the Barracks boundary wall. The buildings date from the1870s but the area is now covered by a public house and leisure complex. (J.G.Simpson)

Sunday timetable -
October 1939 - April 1940

MARKET PLACE AND HARVEY ROAD AND OSMASTON PARK ROAD TO VICTORIA STREET.

Market Place & Harvey Road (Circle) 41	Market Place & Harvey Rd. only 44
Market Place & Brighton Road 42	Victoria St. & Osmaston Park Road (Circle) 31
Market Place & Wyndham St. 45	Victoria St. & Victory Road .. 39

SUNDAYS.

MARKET PLACE VIA LONDON ROAD TO HARVEY ROAD AND OSMASTON PARK ROAD.

9.45 a.m. and every 15 minutes until 1.30 p.m.
1.30 p.m. and every 10 minutes until 5.0 p.m.
5.0 p.m. and every 7½ minutes until 10.15 p.m. (to Harvey Rd. only).
Last through to Osmaston Park Rd. and Victoria St. 10.0 p.m.

HARVEY ROAD TO MARKET PLACE (via London Road).

9.35 and every 15 minutes until 1.35 p.m.
1.47 p.m. and every 10 minutes until 5.17 p.m.
5.22 p.m. and every 7½ minutes until 10.22 p.m.

VICTORIA STREET VIA NORMANTON ROAD TO BARRACKS AND OSMASTON PARK ROAD AND HARVEY ROAD.

9.45 a.m. and every 15 minutes until 1.45 p.m.
1.56 p.m. and every 10 minutes until 4.56 p.m.
5.1 p.m. and every 7½ minutes until 10.16 p.m. (to Osmaston Park Road only).
(Last 'Bus through to Harvey Road 10.1 p.m.).

OSMASTON PARK ROAD (via Barracks) TO VICTORIA STREET.

9.35 a.m. and every 15 minutes until 1.35 p.m.
1.47 p.m. and every 10 minutes until 5.17 p.m.
5.22 p.m. and every 7½ minutes until 10.22 p.m.

→

72. Works specials are depicted in Sinfin Lane. This extension was opened in 1943 as a conversion from motorbuses to accommodate the substantial works traffic during the war period and also to save fuel. To the left is the factory of International Combustion while to the right is F W Hampshire, now part of Reckitt Benckiser. A half mile (0.80km) further on to the rear of the vehicles was a large Ordnance Depot, which has since been developed as industrial units. Brush bodied 193 awaits departure ahead of Sunbeam W 183. (J.G.Simpson)

71. Roe bodied 243 awaits departure from Osmaston Park Road at the Mitre. It has travelled along Harvey Road as route 41, and having crossed Osmaston Road, has then become route 31 to continue along Osmaston Park Road to the Barracks and the town centre via Normanton Road. (R.H.G.Simpson)

→

73. 229 is about to turn round the traffic island at the bottom of Sinfin Lane to reach the stand on the left before returning to town. The Ordnance Depot was in the left background behind 229 and Derby County Football Club's previous training ground to the immediate left. (C.Carter)

LONDON ROAD/
MIDLAND STATION/HARVEY ROAD

74. Semi utility 185 swings round the island at the junction of London Road/Bradshaw Way/Traffic Street inward bound for the Market Place via the Spot and then onwards to Allestree Lane. BICC overhead line hangers have again been used on this installation. (R.Cox)

75. Utility Sunbeam 171 turns out of Midland Road on a depot run. The Midland Station façade at the bottom of the road has since been swept away and replaced by a modern structure. Just behind 171 are the premises of W.W.Winter a Victorian photographer who took many early street scenes of Derby. (C.W.Routh)

76. A busy scene at the junction of Midland Road, from which 216 is emerging, and London Road which again includes 171 this time travelling from Ascot Drive depot to the town centre. Behind 223, to the rear of 171, is St Andrews the "Railwaymen's Church". It was built in stages between 1862/81 to the designs of Gilbert Scott who was retained by the Midland Railway for St Pancras Station. The church included schools, an institute, plus a vicarage and was demolished in 1970/71. (C.J. Barker collection)

77. Having run down Midland Road, Sunbeam W 185 is in Park Street, the first part of the "round the houses" loop to reach the station forecourt. The original intention was to turn in the forecourt but this was refused by L.M.S. This view shows typical Victorian terraced housing complete with corner shop. 185 is on a workman special to take railway workshop workers to Allenton. (J.G.Simpson)

78. 196 finishes the "round the houses" manoeuvre as it leaves Midland Place to cross Railway Terrace to stop in front of the station forecourt. Trolleybuses for Ashbourne Road departed from the opposite side of the road and left via Railway Terrace to the right and thence along Siddals Road to Cockpit Hill. The building to the right is the Railway Institute erected by the Midland Railway for the benefit of its employees. (A.D.Packer)

79. An early view depicts Brush bodied Guy 134 on the Cavendish stand outside the station. It is in "as delivered" tramway style lined out livery. (W.W.Winter)

80. Daimler 161 is on the Allestree Lane stand immediately after the war with station advertising boards still headed LMS (London Midland & Scottish Railway). The Simms van would score at any current day commercial vehicle rally. (W.J.Haynes)

Timetable - April - October 1935

NORMANTON ROUTE.

SUNDAYS.

VICTORIA STREET TO CAVENDISH
9.42 a.m.
9.52 a.m. and every 15 minutes to 1.22 p.m.
1.30 p.m. and every 5 minutes to 11.5 p.m.

CAVENDISH TO VICTORIA STREET
9.55 a.m. and every 15 minutes to 1.40 p.m.
1.52 p.m. and every 5 minutes to 11.12 p.m.

CAVENDISH TO L.M.S. STATION
10.2 a.m. and every 15 minutes to 1.32 p.m.
1.40 p.m. and every 10 minutes to 10.50 p.m.

L.M.S. STATION TO CAVENDISH
10.15 a.m. and every 15 minutes to 1.30 p.m.
1.42 p.m. and every 10 minutes to 11.2 p.m.

WEEKDAYS (MONDAY TO SATURDAY inclusive).

VICTORIA STREET AND CAVENDISH
6.45, 7.0 a.m. and every 10 minutes to 7.40 a.m.   Also 7.15 and 7.27 a.m.
7.40 a.m. and every 5 minutes to 11.5 p.m.

CAVENDISH AND VICTORIA STREET
6.8, 6.55, 7.7, 7.17, 7.27 a.m. and every 5 minutes to 11.17 p.m.
Except 7.57 a.m.

CAVENDISH AND L.M.S. STATION
5.40, 6.20, 6.50, 7.10, 7.15, 7.20, 7.32, 7.40 a.m. and every 10 minutes to 11.0 p.m.

L.M.S. STATION AND CAVENDISH
6.5, 6.35, 7.5, 7.15, 7.22 a.m. and every 10 minutes to 11.12 p.m.

A POSTAL 'BUS will leave the L.M.S. STATION (MONDAY TO FRIDAY) at 9.52 p.m.

Fare chart -April - October 1935

Victoria St., Normanton & L.M.S. Station Route	..	33	L.M.S. Station & Cavendish	..	35
Victoria St. & Cavendish	..	34	Normanton Rd. & Osmaston Rd.		36
			Normanton Rd. & Ashbourne Rd.		32

ORDINARY FARES.

Victoria St. & Moore St.	..	1d.	Cambridge St. & L.M.S. Stn.		1d.
Babington Lane (top) & Normanton Hotel	..	1d.	Victoria St. & St. Thomas' Rd.		1½d.
Moore St. & St. Thomas' Rd.		1d.	Moore St. & Cambridge St...		1½d.
Cavendish & Douglas St.(bottom)		1d.	Cavendish & L.M.S. Station	..	1½d.
Vulcan (Pear Tree) & Bateman St.	.. .. ..	1d.	Victoria St. & L.M.S. Station (via Cavendish)	.. ..	2d.

WORKMEN'S FARES.

Victoria St. & Cambridge St. (via Cavendish)	..	1d.	Victoria St. & L.M.S. Station (via Cavendish)	..	1½d.
Moore St. & L.M.S. Station	..	1d.	Victoria St. & Nightingale Rd. (via Cavendish)	..	1½d.
Moore St. & Nightingale Rd...		1d.	Workmen's Return Fare	..	3d.

TRANSFER FARES.

Normanton Hotel (via Normanton Rd.) to L.M.S. Station .. .. 2d.

81. Moving further along London Road, 208 is about to pass under the overhead junction for Bateman Street. The rear of St Andrews Church can be seen on the left and the warehouse on the right was built for the North Staffordshire Railway when it ran into Derby from Stoke. (R.N.Ashton)

82. 223 has just left London Road and is taking the sharp right hand curve into Bateman Street. London Road continues up the incline to the rear to bridge the Derby to Birmingham railway line and the access lines to the Carriage & Wagon works. (R.N.Ashton)

84. Park Royal bodied Sunbeam W 183 leaves Ascot Drive Depot to travel down to Osmaston Road. This vehicle was delivered in May 1946 and lasted 19 years. (J.G.Simpson)

83. Willowbrook bodied 224 is about to pass under the contact for the automatic switch to continue along London Road; automatic switching always had to be operated for the left hand route in Derby. Behind is Brush bodied 187, which will turn right into Ascot Drive and thence into the depot. (J.G.Simpson)

85. 222 turns out of the northern end of Ascot Drive into London Road to take up service on route 43. Although wired from each end for depot access, Ascot Drive did not have a through trolleybus service. (J.G.Simpson)

86. Sunbeam W 177 with learner driver picks up passengers in what was originally a trolleybus only lane outside the Blue Peter public house Alvaston. This is where the Wyndham Street and Harvey Road routes left the A6 London Road and proceeded along Harvey Road to the right. (C.Carter)

87. A wartime view of Guy 150, complete with masked headlights and white embellishments to assist in the blackout, which is about to turn at Wyndham Street. Note that the word "Derby" has been removed from the vehicle side and the stop sign is a left over from tramway days with "Cars Stop Here" although trams never ran to Wyndham Street. (W.J.Haynes)

OSMASTON ROAD/
ALLENTON/SHELTON LOCK

88. New Years Day 1966 was the official last day of trolleybus operation to Sinfin Lane, although occasional journeys continued for a few months after. 216 turns out of Osmaston Road at Ivy Square into Douglas Street. The overhead junction for Bateman Street is immediately to the rear of the trolleybus on the left. (P.J.Thomas)

89. Turning through 180 degrees and looking along Osmaston Road towards Allenton with 184, 193 and one other trolleybus approaches the Douglas Street junction. The two sets of overhead into Douglas Street from this direction were used by depot workings and works specials. (G.Thomas)

90. We see two of the infamous ex-Hastings Tramways Guy single deckers with 169 (Hastings 38) in the foreground. Six of these vehicles were purchased, but only four entered service, one in 1942 and three in 1943; all were withdrawn by the end of May 1945. The location is the exit roadway from the Osmaston Road Depot. (W.J.Haynes)

91. Two of the trial vehicles seen in a poor state in the period immediately before their withdrawal in 1950. In the foreground is Sunbeam MS2 100 with Ransomes Sims & Jeffries 101 to the rear. The location is again the Osmaston Road Depot exit roadway. (R.Marshall)

92. Sunbeam 202 is on its way to Shelton Lock at the beginning of the factory finishing time. On the right are the Carriage & Wagon workshops and on the left 185 stands with booms down waiting for the influx of workers. Above 185 is the gable end of the Abingdon Street Works, the original 1904 tram depot. Parallel wiring ran from Nightingale Road to Osmaston Road Depot to allow normal service vehicles to pass parked works specials. (R.N.Ashton)

93. The junction for the parallel set of wiring can be seen in this view. Roe bodied 240 is already on the parking loop and is having booms lowered to allow 185 to pass and park further along the road. Nightingale Road, which was the first Rolls Royce site, is to the left rear of 185. (J.G.Simpson)

94. 224 and 207 are under slack overhead at the Nightingale Road turning circle, which was used to turn vehicles before entering the parking loop for Rolls Royce/Carriage & Wagon works specials. The vehicles here are on a National Trolleybus Association tour of the system. The premises to the rear are the builder Ford & Weston's Transport Department. (D.Tate)

95. 224 passes under the Mitre island overhead. The driver required good judgement as all four items of special overhead had insulating dead sections. Trolleybuses were able to turn through 360 degrees around this island and any vehicle travelling from Ascot Drive Depot covered 270 degrees to gain Harvey Road on the right of the picture. Harvey Road trolleybuses turned here before the wiring of Osmaston Park Road. (C.Carter)

96. Chellaston Road, Allenton with 207 depicted in the Allen Street turning circle whilst on an enthusiasts' tour. This was the original terminus of the Osmaston Road route until the extension to Shelton Lock in November 1938. (P.J.Thomas)

97. Roe bodied Sunbeam 240 waits at the Shelton Lock turning circle. The extension from Allenton to Shelton Lock was opened in 1938 and suffered some bomb damage during the war just beyond the Allenton terminus. The actual lock gates were just to the right of the above view and were on the Derby Canal. (C.W.Routh)

GUY

4 & 6-wheeled Trolley Buses

Runback Preventers

No. 6 Feature

In hilly districts runback preventers on tram-cars have been quite common for many years. As the result, however, of GUY Motors' long experience in the manufacture of the trolley buses they found that the ordinary runback preventer is not all that can be desired; for instance, if a driver collapses at the wheel, and the vehicle starts to run backwards down a hill, the ordinary runback preventer only operates when the vehicle has got into such a difficult situation that it has become dewired. A serious accident actually happened some eight years ago, which led to the introduction of the GUY patented system by which the runback preventer comes into immediate operation if the vehicle accidentally runs away, whether it is under the wire or not.

Ask for descriptive literature :

GUY MOTORS LTD., WOLVERHAMPTON.

'Phone : Fallings Park 31421.

London Sales and Service : Porteus Road, Paddington, W.2.

'Phone : Paddington 4492.

Part of a fleet of 62 Guy Trolley Buses in service at Derby.

DEPOTS AND WORKSHOPS

98. 237 on its return journey from Shelton Lock passes the Abingdon Street works. This was the original electric tram depot and workshop opened on the 27th July 1904 and extended in 1906/7. Trolleybuses were maintained here until 1949 when the facility was transferred to Ascot Drive and the building vacated operationally in 1950. (P.J.Thomas)

99. Nottingham Road Depot was opened on 1st February 1909 for electric trams and extended in 1926. With the 1931 opening of Exeter Bridge over the River Derwent there was no tram access to the depot, although track had been laid on one half of the bridge during building to allow the facility to be used well into 1930. It was adapted for trolleybuses ready for the conversion programme, with Nottingham Road being the first route to operate. There was a single entrance on the left, and as the building was single ended, the vehicles turned inside on a loop at the rear of the building before being manoeuvred onto the exit roads. This view is circa 1933 and shows examples of the first three deliveries of Guy BTXs. The depot was closed in September 1949. (C.J.Barker collection)

100. Osmaston Road Depot, which was opened in 1928, had previously been owned by Swinglers Foundry, and prior to that, had been the Victoria and Railway Iron Works. The trolleybus section was a long narrow building with five running roads exiting at the far end. The entrance was through a single doorway opened up in the left side wall. This view circa 1937 shows various Guys over pits, which have guide blocks to ensure no driving mishaps. Trolleybuses ceased operating out of here in 1961 and tower wagons in 1967. (C.J.Barker collection)

101. Utility Sunbeam 171 at the exit to the current Ascot Drive Depot which was purchased in 1947, opened as workshops in June 1949 and as a trolleybus depot in September 1949. There was through running with nine roads plus access to the workshop. (R.F.Mack)

102. 79-84 RC401-406

The first six vehicles were Guy BTXs with Rees Roturbo 75 HP motors and Brush 56 seater bodies. They entered service in January 1932 and were progressively withdrawn between 1946 and 1949. 84 is photographed in winter snow at the early official photograph location just short of the Nottingham Road terminus. The trolley booms have arrester wires and there are front and rearward facing spotlights on the front roof directed towards the overhead. (D.C.O.D.)

103.   **85-92 RC544-551**
       93-98 RC793-798

The next fourteen vehicles were also Guy BTXs with Rees Roturbo 75 HP motors but with Dodson 56 seater bodies. The first eight entered service in July 1932 and the remainder in October/November. All were withdrawn between 1946 and 1949. Here is 88 parked on the south side of Victoria Street still with wartime white stripe on the front panel. If childhood memories are correct these vehicles had rear facing seats behind the lower deck bulkhead. (W.J.Haynes)

104.   **99 RC799**

This was one of the four experimental vehicles and the last produced by Karrier-Clough before this business relationship ceased and Karrier produced trolleybuses in their own right. A Dodson 56 seater body was fitted with power via a BTH 70 HP motor. 99 was not popular with engineering staff and spent long periods out of service between 1938-1943 and 1945-1947. It entered service in December 1932 and was withdrawn in 1951. This shot, on the western side of the Market Place, was in the early years of operation. (C.J.Barker collection)

105. 100 RC800

A second experimental vehicle, which had the same bodybuilder and motor supplier as 99, was a Sunbeam MS2 fitted with Lockheed brakes. It entered service in October 1932 and lasted until 1950. The location of the photograph has not been identified. (C.J.Barker collection)

←

106. 101 RC801

The third trial vehicle was an all Ransomes Sims & Jeffries (RSJ) unit, which first ran in November 1932 and continued in service until 1950. It had a 56 seater body and Allen West/RSJ (70 HP motor) electrical equipment. This photograph is thought to have been taken whilst on trial under Ipswich overhead which was the location of the Ransomes factory.
Rural History Centre, University of Reading)

107. 102-113 RC1102-1113

The next bulk delivery was 12 Guy BTXs with 56 seat Weymann bodies and Rees Roturbo 75 HP motors. These bodies had a less pronounced "piano front", more radiused rear roof and curved lower windscreen. They entered service in July 1933 and were withdrawn between 1946 and 1950. Illustrated is 107 extolling the virtues of Typhoo Tea. (W.W.Winter)

108.   114 RC1414

The fourth trial trolleybus was from the shortlived Brush-Thornycroft business relationship. Thornycroft supplied the chassis but with the motor, electrical equipment and 56 seater body by Brush. It entered service in August 1933 and after a chequered career with many long spells out of service, was withdrawn in 1950. The T of Thornycroft can be clearly seen on the front wheel hub. (Leicestershire Museums)

109.
115-134 RC1615-1634 December 1933 - March 1934	20
135-138 RC2035-2038 July 1934	4
139-144 RC2139-2144 July 1934	6
145-148 RC2645-2648 May/June 1935	4
149-157 RC4349-4357 October & December 1936	9
158 RC4358 July 1937	1
Total	44

44 Guy BTXs with Brush 56 seat bodies delivered in just under four years! 115-148 had Rees Roturbo 75 HP motors whilst 149-158 had Electrical Equipment Company 75 HP motors. First withdrawals were in 1948 with final departures in 1953. 158 was fitted with an experimental braking system. Illustrated is an official view of 146 when new at Kingsway island, Ashbourne Road. (D.C.O.D.)

110. **159-164 RC6659-6664**
Following a 45 day trial in 1937 with Daimler CTM4 demonstrator CWK67, six were ordered and entered service in November/December 1938. They had Metro-Vick 75 HP motors and Brush 54 seat bodies based on a design fitted to Daimler COG5 motorbuses supplied in 1936 and 1938. These were the first two axle trolleybuses and were fitted with traction batteries for off line movement. 161 was withdrawn in 1959 after an accident and the remainder in 1960. (P.J.Thomas collection)

111.   **165-170 DY5113/5115/5123/5137/5140/5584**
      Hastings Fleet Numbers11/13/21/35/38/57
Because of wartime demands, and a lack of new
vehicles, six secondhand single deck Guy BTXs
were purchased from Hastings Tramways in
1942. They were fitted with Rees Roturbo 60
HP motors and central entrance Ransomes Sims
& Jeffries bodies dating from 1928/29. Although
allocated Derby fleet numbers 167 and 170 never
entered service. The four remaining vehicles
entered service between October 1942 and
September 1943. All were withdrawn in 1944/
1945. They were not popular with female drivers
as the spring pressure on the booms was almost
too strong to handle. This view is in Albert Street
opposite the Fish Market with 165 in wartime
livery. (Courtesy of Derby Evening Telegraph)

112.   **171-172 RC8471-8472**
Two vehicles to full wartime utility specification
entered service in July/August 1944. They were
Sunbeam Ws with BTH 85 HP motors and
Weymann 56 seat bodies. Delivered with wooden
slatted seats this wartime feature was changed to
normal upholstered fittings later. Both survived
until 1965 and 172 is preserved and operational
at the Sandtoft Transport Museum. This view is
outside Midland Station; the Weymann bodies
always looked narrower than their later Park
Royal counterparts and were never fitted with
route number boxes. (R.F.Mack)

113. **173-175 RC8573-8575**
     176-185 RC8876-8885
Further deliveries of Sunbeam Ws occurred in 1945 (173-175) and 1946. All were fitted with relaxed utility 56 seater bodies by Park Royal and had BTH 85 HP motors. 173-175 had the front destination indicator in the normal position but were delivered without route number boxes. Two vehicles were subsequently altered but 174 remained without until the end. Two vehicles lasted 20 years with the earliest withdrawal being in 1963 (173). (Derby Museums)

ELECTRIC TROLLEY BUS EQUIPMENT

LOW ENERGY CONSUMPTION PER BUS-MILE

Trolley Bus supplied by The Sunbeam Motor Car Co., Ltd.

BTH Equipment will reduce your running costs on *all* types of Buses

B T H Trolley Bus Motors are virtually indestructible in service, have unsurpassed commutation, and can be wound with ordinary series field, regulated field, or compound field for regenerative control.

B T H Trolley Bus Contactor Control equipments comprise a foot-operated accelerating master controller, contactor panels, unbreakable resistance units, and a manually-operated reverser. Electric braking can be incorporated.

BTH RUGBY

THE BRITISH THOMSON-HOUSTON COMPANY LIMITED, RUGBY, ENGLAND   A.1515.

114.   **186-215 ARC486-515**
The first post war bulk delivery was 30 Sunbeam F4s with Brush 56 seater 8 feet (2.44m) wide bodies and BTH 95 HP motors. Deliveries commenced late in 1948 and were completed by March 1949 allowing the disposal of the early Guy BTXs. 201-215 were fitted with traction batteries. First withdrawals were in 1963 and the final departures in 1967. This photograph was taken at Brush's Loughborough works. (Leicestershire Museums)

115. **216-235 DRC216-235**

A further 20 Sunbeam F4s were delivered in 1952/53 but this time with Willowbrook 60 seater bodies based on the Brush design; Brush received the original order. They had BTH 95 HP motors and 216 was exhibited at the 1952 Commercial Motor Show. All were withdrawn in 1967 with the closure of the system although it is still possible to ride on 224 at the East Anglian Transport Museum near Lowestoft.
(Willowbrook)

116. **236-243 SCH236-243**

The final batch of trolleybuses was 6 Sunbeam F4As with Roe 65 seat bodies and AEI 95 HP motors. 236 was originally fitted with automatic acceleration equipment. Delivery was in the first half of 1960 and they lasted just over seven years before closure of the system. They were extremely handsome vehicles with a good turn of speed. 236 moves around the southwestern corner of the Market Place to regain the Shelton Lock stand; it was exhibited at the 1959 Commercial Motor Show. (J.G.Simpson)

*If model makers wish to see line drawings of the vechicles operated in Derby, there is the Park Royal bodied Sunbeam W in **Maidstone Trolleybuses** and the single deck Guy in **Hastings Trolleybuses**.*

TOWER WAGONS

117. Crossley Tower Wagon No1 (originally No4) was converted from one of the three trial diesel single deckers, which entered service in January 1935. It was hired to the War Department and purchased by them in April 1941. It was repurchased in July 1943, shortened and fitted with a tower from an earlier vehicle. When scrapped in 1957 the tower was again transferred to a Daimler motorbus conversion to make Tower Wagon No5. (R.G.H.Simpson)

118. One of the three Daimler COG5 motorbuses converted to tower wagons by the department. No2 was originally 52 delivered in 1936 and converted in 1951 using a tower from an earlier vehicle. The callout is to a section of Kedleston Road. (R.F.Mack)

THE BEGINNING AND THE END

119. A composite picture published in the local paper on the 8th April 1930 giving a foretaste of things to come. The vehicle on the right is Bradford 572 from the first bulk delivery of double deckers for that city produced by English Electric in 1929. The vehicle on the left is Wolverhampton 53, which was a Guy BTX with Dodson body delivered in 1928. (Courtesy of Derby Evening Telegraph)

120. The morning after the night before! Willowbrook bodied Sunbeams parked at the side of Ascot Drive Depot after closure of the system with number plates removed awaiting collection by the dealers; 15 of the batch of 20 went for scrap to Askin of Barnsley. Trolleybuses served Derby for over 35 years, including the difficult war years, so it is perhaps fitting that the destinations have been wound to display Nottingham Road Cemetery. (R.F.Mack)

MP Middleton Press

Easebourne Lane, Midhurst, W Sussex. GU29 9AZ Tel: 01730 813169 Fax: 01730 812601
*If books are not available from your local transport stockist, order direct with cheque,
Visa or Mastercard, post free UK.*